A Place to Talk *in* Extended Schools

'It's true, sometimes we just can't see the wood for the trees. Not only does Elizabeth Jarman provide the inspiration and incentive for early years education and childcare practititioners to stop, look and take stock, she demonstrates how both the wood and the trees can be used to create magical thinking spaces that can't fail to be irresistible to children and adults alike!'

Kay Errington, Early Years Service Manager
Bournemouth Borough Council

A Place to Talk *in*
Extended Schools

Elizabeth Jarman

Reprinted 2009
Published 2009 by A&C Black Publishers Limited
36 Soho Square, London W1D 3QY
www.acblack.com

First published 2007 by Featherstone Education Limited

ISBN 978-1-9060-2928-9

Text © Elizabeth Jarman
Photographs © Elizabeth Jarman

A CIP record for this publication is available from the British Library.

Printed in Great Britain by Martins the Printers Ltd

This book is produced using paper that is made from wood grown in
managed, sustainable forests. It is natural, renewable and recyclable.
The logging and manufacturing processes conform to the environmental
regulations of the country of origin.

To see our full range of titles
visit www.acblack.com

Introduction

The recent I CAN report[1] suggests that over 50% of children in England are starting school with some form of speech and language difficulty or disability. However, we recognise that "communication is the foundation life skill of the 21st century."[2] Improving children's speaking and listening skills, has never been so important and we all have a role to play.

This resource considers the significant role that the physical environment can play in supporting children's speaking and listening skills; in supporting inquisitive, verbal experimentation, not just answering questions!

It includes a summary of some of the key environmental influences, collated from research studies; it includes lots of examples of what this looks like in practice; it poses questions to prompt action and it sign-posts you to further information.

We hope that the resource will challenge and inspire practitioners working in Extended Schools to create some really effective 'places to talk'.

[1] *Cost to the Nation,* I CAN, 2006

[2] I CAN website www.ican.org.uk

A Place to Talk *in* Extended Schools

Contents

A Place to Talk *in* Extended Schools

Five environmental factors to consider

Following a review of research and practice in Early Years settings across England and Wales, we have identified five really important environmental points to consider when creating spaces designed to encourage children's speaking and listening skills.

1. *The physical environment should reflect the pedagogy[3] of the setting.*

Establishing a shared team understanding of your pedagogy will inform the way that you plan your learning environment. The way that a physical space is arranged says a lot to children about what is expected there and the sort of interactions welcome. It's really important that the learning environment and pedagogy connect and support one another.

2. *Practitioners should make the most of the space available, both inside and out.*

It's important to view learning spaces as a whole, including both inside and out and make the most of what's available. Across the space, children need secure spaces to talk where they feel comfortable and relaxed.

3. *Spaces should take account of physical factors that can impact on learning; for example, noise, colour and light.*

Noise

Being in a noisy environment makes it really difficult for children to concentrate. This can have a negative effect on their speaking and listening skills.

Colour

Colours need to be chosen carefully as they can affect children's behaviour and ability to focus and engage in conversation.

[3] *pedagogy* is your 'teaching' style

Light

Current research confirms that we are all energized by natural sunlight and that children learn faster in spaces with natural light. Light can be used to create mood and define an area.

4. The environment should not be over stimulating.

Too much choice can be overwhelming. Storage options should therefore be carefully considered.

The purpose and positioning of displays needs review. For example, it makes sense not to have a busy, cluttered display in an area where children are expected to focus say on a story book at group time.

5. Spaces should be viewed from the child's perspective.

Informed by a thorough understanding of how language develops we should keenly observe what the children are actually doing and how they are responding to the spaces we create, in order to plan appropriate, flexible environments that stimulate speaking and listening skills.

Twelve ideas to try

Inspired by practice from many settings, we have created twelve 'places to talk' that reflect the five environmental factors.

Each idea is spread over two pages:

➢ There is a 'starter' photograph of the space and a description of how we created it.

➢ We have included key points about why we chose those particular materials, why we positioned the furniture as we did and so on.

➢ There are also some photographs of children using the space, with their comments and some observations of what they did.

➢ We have included some action points for you to consider.

You'll see that what we are talking about does not have to cost a fortune, in fact you may already have some of the materials and resources that we have used. What it does involve though, is an informed view, keen observation skills which inform planning, so that you create the sort of environment that reflects what you want for children in your setting.

We acknowledge that opportunities for speaking and listening are everywhere, and we hope that these ideas will inspire you to review and develop some special 'places to talk' in your setting.

A quiet space to withdraw and reflect

How and why?

This space was created using garden canes, a long piece of lacy material attached with pegs and then filled with soft, textured cushions and blankets.

The outside area where we set up this space was very busy. We wanted to offer the children somewhere to retreat to, to reflect and to chat. The see through material allowed them to still see what was going on in the garden. The textures in the material and cushions added softness to the space and a feeling of homeliness.

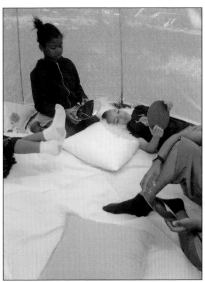

We added some small mirrors to the space and this triggered lots of language and games of looking at each other. The calmness that this space created allowed the children to use quieter voices and to engage in descriptive, more considered language.

The group really enjoyed being in this enclosed, safe space. They spent a long time chatting, lying down and resting. Spaces like this, which encourage children to relax and reflect are so important, especially at the end of a school day, when they may well be tired.

"This space took hardly any time to set up and the resources used need hardly any storage space. The children loved it." (Brid)

Action

Do you have any 'soft' spaces in your environment where children can relax and reflect? Think about how you could adapt this idea to suit your setting.

Negotiation

How and why?

This space was set up in an extended school of sixty children, based in a school hall. We wanted to create small spaces to add more privacy. Children respond well to small spaces that they can 'get into'.

Simply using two big cardboard boxes, positioned to face one another, to encourage interaction and a couple of soft blankets was all it took!

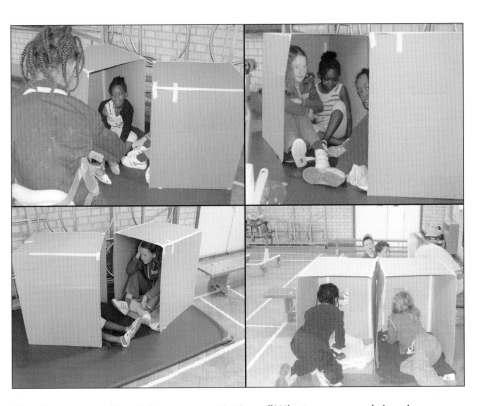

Small spaces often trigger negotiation. "What are you doing in there?" "Can I come in?" The three girls 'got in' and closed the boxes to make a really private, enclosed space. They whispered for a long time and then made windows in each box to interact with the boys in the zone next to them. The boxes only lasted for a day but they were free, stimulated such a lot of language and gave this particular group tremendous fun!

Action

If you run your extended school in a hall, take a moment to think about the environment from the child's point of view. How could you create some semi-private quiet spaces for just one or two?

A place for one

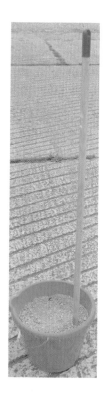

How and why?

Here is an example of a space for one. We created this space using a folding table and stool. Using folding equipment was important due to limited storage. We made the screening from a long piece of netting attached by pegs onto 'bucket supports'. These were made by putting ready mix concrete in buckets and adding a broom handle. We left them over night to set. We then had really flexible supports to use inside and out.

Adding screening is important to help children to concentrate more deeply as it removes the often distracting influences that interrupt thinking, for example the flow of movement.

"We use the bucket supports all the time now. They are really sturdy and so flexible. We've noticed a difference - before the children were easily distracted when people walked or ran by. The screens help to reduce this." (Linda)

Action

Review the spaces in your setting. Think about the flow of movement and how this can impact on children who are trying to concentrate. What resources do you already have that could create a simple screening system, to reduce distractions and help children focus more deeply?

An enclosed space

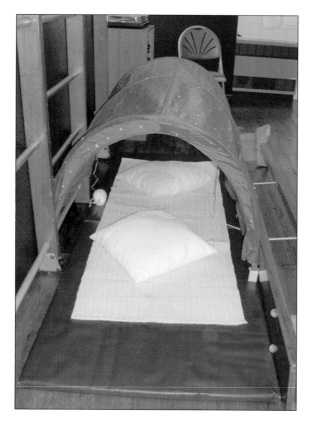

How and why?

This pop up tunnel structure, with a mat, night light and finger puppets created an enclosed space at the side of the hall. The space was quick to create and took up little storage space. The night light added a magical feel and the comfy flooring and cushions offered the children an alternative context for story making.

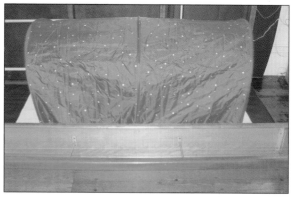

"I like it in here. It's cool. It's a nice place to sit." (Katherine)

Action

Do you have pop up structures to create instant spaces? Look out for them in shops and garden centres. They are cheap, easy to assemble and take up little storage space.

Using existing structures

How and why?

This small space was created really easily and in minutes. We used a sheet, pegs and cushions. We positioned two 'A frames' on a soft mat and enclosed them with the sheet. We used blue cushions - blue is a calming, tranquil colour. The sheet is neutral, so it doesn't distract the children and the feeling of enclosure allows them to focus more deeply on what they are doing.

A Place to Talk *in* Extended Schools

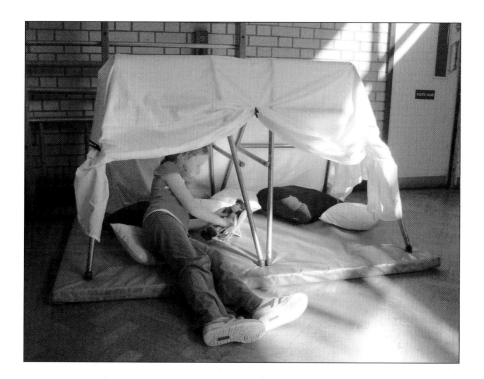

"I like it in here because it's quiet and I can talk to my doll without everyone hearing me." (Shauna)

"This reminds me of the sort of spaces we used to make when we were children. Using everyday things makes this approach possible for everyone." (Tom)

Action

How can you make use of existing structures in your setting to easily create small spaces for children to talk?

An instant reading corner

How and why?

Unable to leave resources out, this setting put up several hooks so that they can create spaces quickly. We used material to define this space. Loops had been sewn onto the fabric so that it could be quickly 'hooked up' onto the wall. The logs and textured cushions offered various seating options and the small selection of books in wicker baskets allowed the children a manageable amount of choice.

The children liked this space and used it as a base to share books and conversations together. The natural materials like the logs, added to the discussion and exploration of the space, appealing to the senses - the feel, smell and look of the logs.

Action

The logs were free. Logs or rocks can add a new dimension to spaces, stimulating talk and if arranged in groups, offering children places to naturally gather. How could you use natural materials in your outside space?

A temporary space

How and why?

This pop up tent is quite unusual because of it's pale colour - they are usually bold, bright, primary colours. The pale colour really helps children to be calm, to concentrate and to relax. This space was created in minutes and offered a quiet space in a busy outside area. The rug was 'bobbly' and added an interesting texture.

"They won't fit. I've got it stuck!" said Kisa.

The boxes added interest to the space, acting as a provocation, stimulating talk and thinking.

"These tents take up no space and offer quiet areas in our busy setting. It's interesting watching which children spend time in them - often it's the timid ones who need to feel safe when they're outside." (Tom)

Action

Could you use tents to create temporary spaces in your setting? How and where?

Willow structures: build your own!

How and why?

This setting wanted to involve the children in developing some structures in their outside area. They created these structures with the help of an expert, during a workshop session. This offered a lovely activity for children and staff together, stimulated lots of discussion and gave the opportunity to work with a natural and unusual medium - willow.

Planting willow in the spring time quickly creates a leafy, living structure, perfect for children to retreat to for quiet times.

The structures here were planted in the summer months and will have climbers added to give that semi-private feel.

"*Involving the children with this project was a great start to our summer scheme. Learning new skills together gave us so much to talk about. We all enjoyed building and the children are really enjoying using the areas they created for a range of communication based activities.*" (Sue)

Action

How could you use structures like these in your space?

A small reading tent in an outside area designed to encourage children to relax and spend time enjoying books

How and why?

We created this space using: a draped tent, a couple of circular mats, some beige cushions and a wicker box. We chose the quietest space available and made use of the existing fencing to support the tent.

This space offers a contained, calm area for a small number of children to retreat to within an often busy outside space.

"We like it when we close the curtains. We can see out. It's nice in here." (Oliver)

"It's really important for us to plan spaces where children can spend time alone or with a small group. They don't want to be part of a big group the whole time." (Brid)

Action

Where could you create a small temporary space in your setting? How could you position spaces so that you take advantage of the naturally quiet areas?

A space tucked away in a cupboard!

How and why?

It's so important to maximise the use of space and use every nook and cranny available. This cupboard when emptied of storage units and boxes, offered a small space, tucked away from the general noise and activity of the setting. We added a door hanging to give a private feel to the space and a string of white lights to give the cupboard a different feel to the main hall.

The selection of seasonal materials to explore, triggered lots of descriptive language. We also added a short drape to cover the distracting trays of materials in the top part of the cupboard.

A Place to Talk *in* Extended Schools

"These are compacted. I don't know why they are all different shapes."

"This is my favourite space. It's quite private. I like the lights and just playing with the conkers." (Amber)

"Children need spaces like this to unwind, think and be quiet. We often make the mistake of assuming they want to be 'on the go' in big groups all the time. I know that I like to spend time on my own sometimes- so why shouldn't they?" (Penny)

Action

What spaces could you use to create small spaces for thinking and being quiet? What about using a storage cupboard, once you have removed the resources you are using, or an alcove?

A hideaway tent

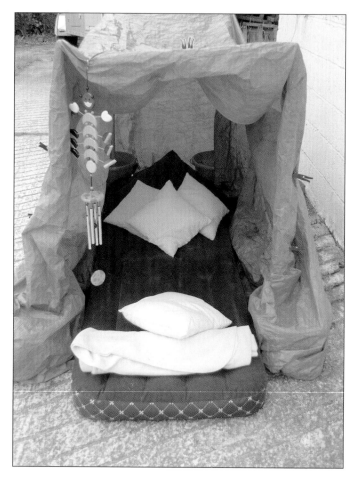

How and why?

We used the bucket supports and a tarpaulin to create this space on a rainy day. It's important to have a collection of different types of materials so that you can create areas whatever the weather. We added a blow up mattress and some cushions for the children to crawl onto. The wind chime added a sense of calm to the space and attracted the children's listening skills.

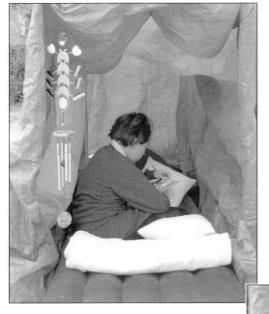

The space was used by different children, some reading magazines, others experimenting with the chime. All of the children liked the spaces away from the busy activities outside and the time alone.

At one point it rained and two children sheltered inside. "We can hear all the rain. It's like we are in the shower but we're not getting wet."

"We hadn't thought of using spaces outside in wet weather. Getting waterproof materials like these make that possible. It gets so noisy inside when it's a wet day, creating a few spaces like this outside near the door could be fun and also offer quiet spots." (Linda)

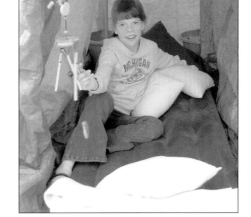

Action

What sort of spaces could you create in your outside area if it rains?

Consultation: what kind of spaces do you like?

How and why?

Children have preferences about spaces. They like creating their own areas. We gave this group a choice of materials and resources, some cups and a jug of juice and asked them to make a space where they could enjoy their drink. They worked as a team, chose a shady location under a tree, tried really hard to fix the net onto the tree, using pegs, ties and lots of imagination. There was a huge amount of discussion and negotiation. It was a real challenge with purpose.

A Place to Talk *in* Extended Schools

"We'd not thought about asking the children to show us what sort of spaces they like. They have some great ideas." (Linda)

"It'd be well good if we could do walls and an upstairs." (Leon)

"It's our place." (Daniel)

Action

What sort of materials and fixings could you offer children so that they can create their own spaces? Consider developing collections of 'den making' resources.

Action points to consider

Here is a summary of the questions we posed to prompt action. Use them to reflect on the environment that you currently provide for children and then to help you focus on making positive changes.

➤ Walk through your setting. Do you have any 'soft' spaces where children can relax?

➤ How could you create some semi-private spaces for just one or two?

➤ Think about the flow of movement and how this can impact on children who are trying to concentrate. What resources do you already have that could create a simple screening system, to help children focus more deeply?

➤ Do you have pop up structures to create instant spaces?

➤ How can you make use of existing structures in your setting to easily create small spaces for children to talk?

➤ How could you use natural materials in your outside space?

➤ Where could you create a small temporary space to support learning in your setting?

➤ How can you position spaces so that you take advantage of the naturally quiet areas?

➤ Where could you create small spaces?

➤ What sort of spaces could you create in your outside area if it rains?

➤ What sort of materials and fixings could you offer children so that they can create their own spaces?

➤ What's your role in supporting children's speaking and listening skills?

Useful resources

The resources that we used to create our 'places to talk' were easy to source and inexpensive. They included:

➢ Net curtains

➢ Blankets in natural, relaxing colours

➢ Textured cushions

➢ Different sized rugs

➢ Interesting objects to stimulate talk eg smoothe stones, knarled wood, conkers

➢ Drapes to diffuse light

➢ Strings of lights

➢ Lamps

➢ Low furniture

➢ A folding table and stool

➢ Garden canes

➢ Packing boxes

➢ A sheet

➢ Pegs

➢ Baskets

Further references and useful websites

The Communication Friendly Spaces Toolkit: Improving Speaking and Listening Skills in the Early Years Foundation Stage. Jarman, Elizabeth (2007). ISBN: 1-859-90428-9. Can be ordered from Prolog (0870 600 2400)

Cost to the Nation, I CAN, 2006, available from www.ican.org.uk

www.pge.com for information about studies on the way day lighting affects children's learning

www.sightlines-initiative.com for information about the Reggio Emilia Children's Network, conferences and resources

www.quietclassrooms.org for guidance on controlling noise in settings and public places

www.colourtest.ue-foundation.org for information on the effects of colours on behaviour

Children, Spaces, Relations: Meta project for an environment for young children, Ceppi, G; Zini, M. (1998) Reggio Children Publications. ISBN: 8-887-96011-9

www.continyou.org.uk/extendedschools for information, resources and case studies about the extended schools support service

A Place to Talk *in* Extended Schools

Other books in this series

A Place to Talk: Children's Centres
978 1 906029 27 2

A Place to Talk: Pack-away Settings
978 1 906029 26 5

A Place to Talk: Pre-schools
978 1 906029 25 8

all by Elizabeth Jarman